PROJECT MANAGEMENT FOR ARCHIVISTS

PROJECT MANAGEMENT FOR ARCHIVISTS

Befriending Your Backlog

Kelly Spring

East Carolina University

Suggested citation: Spring, Kelly. Project Management for Archivists:
Befriending Your Backlog.

doi: https://doi.org/10.5149/9781469661261_Spring

ISBN 978–1-4696–6125–4 (cloth: alk. paper)
ISBN 978–1-4696–6126–1 (open access ebook)

CONTENTS

1 WELCOME!

3 GETTING TO KNOW YOUR BACKLOG
3 Scope and Inventory
3 New Material and Provenance
4 Tools
5 Method

7 FINDING YOUR BASELINE
7 Identifying Minimum Requirements
7 Baseline Components: Intellectual
8 Baseline Components: Physical

11 ACHIEVING YOUR BASELINE
11 Avoiding the Shiny
11 Creating Checklists

17 STRATEGIZING
17 Balance
17 Creating a Workflow

23 KEEPING TRACK
23 Project Plans
23 Benchmarks
24 Scalability

This handbook is intended to aid practitioners in knowing where to begin and how to move forward on systematically mastering an archival backlog. Briefly covered here are creating inventories, defining baseline standards, developing guides, and assembling workflows. It is project management for archival . . . well, projects, and it will keep an archivist from getting bogged down in the details.

Ordinarily, general project management focuses on the details needed for one project. With a backlog, however, each collection becomes its own project. Therefore, it is important to develop a method for managing all of them in aggregate. Often, the word *backlog* conjures images of never-been-touched material needing accessioning, but repositories can just as easily have a list of accessioned material needing processing or a conglomerate of digitization needs. A backlog may refer to any accumulation of uncompleted work. This handbook focuses on archival accessioning over any other task; however, the principles may easily be applied to processing, cataloging, digitizing, or dealing with born-digital collections.

The depth of information included here is limited. Many archivists have written books on managing, arranging, describing, and caring for archival material in all formats. My intention is to give you a small, simple resource to guide you in the right direction. I hope that you'll find this handbook useful.

Kelly Spring

Scope and Inventory

At the beginning of any project, it's important to define its scope. What information do you want to capture and how much of your time can you expend getting it? For example, maybe there are carts in the workroom filled with unrecorded donations that you'd like a better handle on. If you are a lone arranger, you have precious little time to look in-depth at each donation. So, you will want to make a broad sweep of the carts, jotting down general notes on the type of material, the amount of material, and where it all came from.

If the stack space is in relatively good shape, though, perhaps a systematic way to process accessions is all that's needed. In that case, you'll be tracking accession numbers and priority rankings. Possibly, too, you'd like a snapshot of legacy digital media hiding in your collections. To carry that out it will be necessary to document collection number, box number, and type of media found within your materials.

In thinking about your goals, you will naturally define the scope by listing the smallest information points needed. These points will help shape a full inventory of the materials in your backlog. Start simple. There will be further opportunities to expand on the information that you initially record. For now, focus on getting to know the entire perspective of your backlog.

New Material and Provenance

Provenance, according to the Society of American Archivists glossary, refers to the individual, family, or organization that created or received the items in a collection. In creating an inventory for un-accessioned material, keep items created or collected by the same individual or group together. Sometimes (and sometimes often!), the provenance information simply does not exist, and the archivist must do a little research to discern the origin of the material.

At other times, you may find it necessary to group items according to other criteria, such as with zine collections or advertising ephemera.

If creating an inventory of accessioned material, you may want to group things according to priority or collecting area to better facilitate processing strategies; and if creating an inventory of accessioned born-digital content slated for disk imaging, one option is to group items according to format. No matter how the material is sorted, understanding your backlog in larger groupings helps maintain the connections between interrelated items while allowing the archivist to more easily gain an overarching view of the material.

Tools

Creating an inventory is as easy as picking up a pencil and notepad, but most choose to enter information into a spreadsheet.

Date of inventory entry.	Generally speaking, what is it?	Where did it come from?	Date the material arrived?	Are there any names associated with the material?	Where is the material currently located?

Simple = scalable

Sample of a simple inventory spreadsheet

Mobile applications such as Google Keep and Google Forms are an alternative when working with assistants and volunteers because, provided a Wi-Fi connection, they can take a cell phone or tablet directly into the area being inventoried. These programs are web-based, allow attaching photographs of the material directly to notes or inventory entries, and have built-in export features for transforming the data to other formats when needed.

Method

Make an entry for each group of items that make up your backlog. Work systematically from area to area in all office and storage locations where the material is kept. Be sure to include items found on shelves, in file cabinets, in desks, behind doors, and so on. If backlog items are located in off-site storage, add that to your inventory. For born-digital material, methodically check physical storage locations for media carriers, hard drives, network drives, and cloud storage for electronic files.

- **Basic characteristics of an accessioning inventory**
- Description
- Current housing
- Extent (i.e., how many containers to look for)
- Current location
- Provenance
- Relevant information written on the containers

- **Basic characteristics of an inventory for processing or otherwise working with cataloged material**
- Name of the accession/collection
- Unique identifier
- Approximate priority
- Current location

But . . .

What if there isn't any identifying information on the container? Or what if the information on the box doesn't match the contents?

Take a cursory glance at the material and use sticky notes, index cards, or scrap paper to write any general descriptive information possible. Resist the temptation to go into too much detail. If it's a particularly challenging item and it's unclear what it is or where it came from, indicate that as well. Then securely affix the notes to the boxes. You could write directly on the boxes, however, it is possible that you end up with a lot of crossed out information on each box leaving you to wonder what information is correct or the most up-to-date. Tagging the containers in this way has the added benefit of marking physical progress on your inventory.

What if I can't complete the inventory in one session?

This is totally normal. Include in your inventory the date of entry and your name or initials, indicate on the physical material that it has been accounted for, and move in an orderly fashion. These tips should make it easier to pick up where you left off.

Identifying Minimum Requirements

Now that you have an inventory and can better see the entirety of the backlog, the next step is to find the absolute minimum that needs to be done across all groups that you've identified. This will provide you with a baseline.

An accessioning baseline is the least amount of work required to gain physical and intellectual control of your archival holdings. A processing baseline expands on that to encompass increased intellectual control as well as public access. Baselines for born-digital material are as simple as documenting the existence and location of material or as robust as creating multiple copies and access points, and a digitization baseline will focus on the quality of the digital surrogate and amount of metadata. What works for one institution, however, may not fit with another. Scope out the baseline in concert with the needs of your project and the needs of your repository.

Baseline Components: Intellectual

Think for a moment about the user. Will your user be staff (as in processing) or public (as in research)? What information will they need to take the next actionable step in their work? When dealing solely with acquisitions, the user is likely a colleague, intern, or volunteer assisting with future processing. What knowledge will they need to get started on that processing project without having to backtrack and without having most of the work already completed? If already at the processing stage, your user is most likely the researcher. In this case, the user may need only enough information to decide whether to pursue looking at a collection.

A common starting point for developing an intellectual baseline is DACS (Describing Archives Content Standard). Published by the Society of American Archivists, it outlines "discrete descriptive elements [that] convey standardized information about the archival materials and creators being described."

For example, the title or the reference code (the collection's unique identifier). A full list of the DACS minimum requirements is below:

- Reference Code (DACS 2.1)
- Name and Location of Repository (DACS 2.2)
- Title (DACS 2.3)
- Date (DACS 2.4)
- Extent (DACS 2.5)
- Name of Creator(s) (DACS 2.6)
- Scope and Content (DACS 3.1)
- Conditions Governing Access (DACS 4.1)
- Languages and Scripts of the Material (DACS 4.5)

The ISAD(G) (General International Standard Archival Description) is another resource to draw from when devising an intellectual baseline. It outlines twenty-six (26) elements used in an archival finding aid, six (6) of which are considered essential, including the level of description and appraisal information. These are:

- Reference Code (ISAD(G) 3.1.1)
- Title (ISAD(G) 3.1.2)
- Date (ISAD(G) 3.1.3)
- Extent (ISAD(G) 3.1.5)
- Name of Creator(s) (ISAD(G) 3.2.1)
- Level of Description (ISAD(G) 3.1.4)

Baseline Components: Physical

The physical baseline applies to the handling of the actual material in order to ease tracking and provide any preservation needs. The elements in the physical baseline are more task-focused and orient toward collections maintenance and environmental control.

Examples of collections maintenance elements include rehousing the material when the current housing is insufficient and labeling the containers. Environmental control elements include finding shelf space for the material and tracking or documenting locations.

Baselines and the inhomogeneous nature of archives

When archival materials are not alike and cannot be described in the same way, it can seem conflicting to apply a uniform standard to everything in your project. While it's true that one set of records will not have the exact qualities as another, there will be enough similarities to enable the use of a systematic guideline across the collections in your repository. It is okay if you feel like you're going against your natural inclination to offer the best description possible. Remember that you are looking to cut your backlog through iteration. During future iterations of your project, be it processing or other tasks, there will be opportunities to create a more full and complete description.

Baseline examples from other institutions:

University of California, Irvine (UCI)
UCI creates a collection-level record for all holdings and posts a minimal finding aid to the Online Archive of California for every collection, regardless of processing status. Therefore, UCI's baseline elements come from a mix of what was traditionally thought of as separate accessioning and processing phases.

East Carolina University (ECU)
ECU also creates a collection-level record for all holdings and posts a minimal finding aid to their website for every collection, regardless of processing status. But ECU approaches accession numbers a little differently. The identifiers consist of the collection number followed by a sequential number (123.002). This requires that a collection number be assigned to every new acquisition that is not an accretion to an existing collection.

Avoiding the Shiny

Within every backlog are glittering gems that can distract and pull the unsuspecting archivist off course. The photographs documenting buildings that once stood in your town or World War II letters that portray a young couple's love story are easily captivating. In our line of work, we are fortunate to find such treasures and we should enjoy that aspect of our career, but we also need to share the resources with others. So, to ensure that you meet the minimum requirements of your project in a systematic and reliable way across all material, you'll want to have a checklist.

A checklist outlines the steps necessary to put a baseline into action. What tasks will formally identify and record the information in your minimum standard? Are administrative components inherent to the process? For example, creating a collection file facilitates administrative control of the collection and is assumed as part of accessioning, yet it most likely doesn't appear in the baseline. This document will help in managing know-how, or the practical knowledge on getting things done.

Creating Checklists

Checklists seem simple enough that the value of having one could easily be overlooked. A good checklist is precise, efficient, and easy to use even in the most difficult situations and its use will improve performance and aid in achieving consistent results.

Creating a unique checklist for yourself or your institution is an important exercise because it gives you ownership of the process. You may wish to customize an existing checklist or you might prefer to start from scratch. Here are some examples:

Accessioning Checklist

Immediate fate of accession (in consultation with University Archivist)

Will this accession be processed immediately? If yes, skip this section. If no, follow additional steps below.	☐Yes ☐No
Create instances and barcoded top containers for all boxes	☐
Scan barcode sheets and add to accession folder with name convention *accessionNumber-barcodes.pdf*	☐
Enter Horizon number in the user defined field Bib Number	☐
Include Processing Plan under Collection Management	☐

AS Basic Information section

Evaluate the physical condition of the accession and record a Condition Description note if accession is in less than Good condition	☐
Enter information in accessions restrictions note (use ALT+R to access macro)	☐
Determine whether there are use restrictions, if applicable check use restrictions and enter information in use restrictions note (Ex. donor agreement indicates something cannot be digitized or reading room access only for digital collections)	☐ N/A: ☐

AS Dates section

Enter date (mandatory) and date expression (optional)	☐

Archivists' Toolkit Accessioning Checklist, p. 1. Johns Hopkins University. Jordon Steele.

Collection Title:	
Collection Number:	
Accession Number:	

Accessioned by:	Start Date:	End Date:

Accessioning Tasks Completed

Date

Determine accession number and create new accession record in AS		YYYY/MM/DD
Rebox/refolder collection for stabilization/preservation (if needed)		YYYY/MM/DD
Complete accession record in AT:	**Check tasks with an "X"**	
		YYYY/MM/DD
Title		
Identifier (Accession Number)		
Date accessioned		
Description		
Condition description		
Disposition Note (if needed)		
Inventory		
General note		
Acquisition type		
Resource type		
Restrictions Apply (if needed)		
Access Restrictions (only check if restrictions)		
Access Restrictions Note		
Use Restrictions (if needed)		
Use Restrictions Note (if needed)		
Date		
Extent number		
Container Summary		
Agent links (creator / source)		
Related resources		

Accession Checklist, p. 1. University of California, Irvine. Author unknown.

Name:

Date:

Merritt Metadata

- **Title:** *[Collection Name. EX: J. Hillis Miller disk images and digital files]*
- **Creator:** *[Creating entity. Follow LOC authority where possible. EX: Miller, J. Hillis]*
- **Date:** *[OPTIONAL. May be changed after LAMMP processing reveals dates last modified. EX: 1961-2013]*
- **Collection Number:** *[Collection #. EX: MS-C013]*
- **Accession Number:** *[Accession #. EX: AS-169_2015.003]*
- **Value Score:** *[Use matrix for LAMMP Value Score. Not applicable to purely born digital material]*

Type and Extent

Material on Digital Media Carriers(s): Number of items and approximate capacity in bytes of physical media carriers. For extremely large accessions of born-digital media, approximate the number of items.

Purely Digital Material: Number of directories & files with capacity of highest level directories, along with known/best guess of creating OS.

Naming Convention

Material on Digital Media Carriers(s): Print labels with digital object # for each piece of digital media, then note range of labels here first to last. EX: MSC013_DIG001 – MSC013_DIG448

Purely Digital Material: Table of directories/content to include in each LAMMP object along with corresponding digital object #. See example below.

Content	Digital Object #
Desktop/	*MSF029_DIG001*
Documents/, My Pictures/, Users/	*MSF029_DIG002*
File 1, File 2, File 3, etc.	*MSF029_DIG003*
...	...

Born-Digital Materials Accessioning Form. University of California, Irvine. Laura Uglean Jackson and Matthew McKinley.

ARCHIVAL COLLECTION ACCESSION CHECKLIST for CURATORS

Collection Title: _____
[AS = Title]
If this is an addition to an existing collection, enter the collection title. If this is an accession for an entirely new collection, enter the name associated with the collection and the type of material. (Examples: Brad Brafford papers; Alice Hupert photographs.)

[AS = Identifier] _____
This will be an accession number that the archivist assigns. For example 2016 028 where 2016 is the calendar year and 028 is the number of the accession. In AS, enter the year in the first box and the number in the second.

[AS = Accession Date]
Will usually be today's date.

Description:_____
_____
_____
_____
_____

[AS = Content Description]
Include one or two sentences about the creator that would provide context for the materials. Also include information about the content and format(s) of the materials:

Condition Description: _____
_____

[AS = Condition Description]
Include information about the physical condition of the materials, such as whether paper is brittle or torn, whether magnetic media are deteriorating, and any other concerns. Notify the archivist if you encounter serious ongoing preservation concerns such as bugs or mold!!

Accession Checklist for Curators, p. 1. University of California, Irvine. Kelly Spring.

Sequence

For accessioning and processing checklists, begin by looking at your archival management system. Pay attention to the order in which the data entry fields appear in the management system and align your checklist to that exact order for ease of use. If creating a born-digital accessioning or processing checklist, review the sequence outlined in your disk imaging or forensic software. Similarly, for digitization or reformatting checklists, look to your asset management system for the correct order of events.

Tasks

While you were looking at the data entry sequence you may have already started to flesh out your checklist. Now you'll refer to your baseline and make sure that the elements are somehow represented in your checklist. Add any missing elements in the correct order on the checklist.

There will be extra tasks to undertake in order to meet some of the baseline requirements. For example, in processing a collection an archivist must actually create the resource record (i.e., open a new, blank record) before the elements "abstract" and "finding aid title" can be completed. So, if the archivist is using Archivist's Toolkit or ArchivesSpace, "spawn resource record" is added as a task to their processing checklist. Consider the additional tasks you'll need and add them to your checklist.

- **Sample checklist items include**
- Begin new accession record in archival database
- Assign an identifier to the accession
- Assess the condition of the material
- Document the extent of the accession
- Enter a description of the accession
- Indicate if born-digital material is included
- Assign processing priority
- Assign the material a location

Review

Finally, review the checklist and rearrange any tasks that seem out of order. Repeat as necessary.

Balance

When faced with a backlog, a workflow will give you more consistent results and will help you and your staff better manage the time it takes to complete each task. It will also let everyone know exactly where and when in the process to hand off the work. A workflow is essentially your checklist in motion. It takes the tasks from your checklist and assigns them to the people who will carry them out.

Creating a Workflow

Listing roles

Make a list of team members. This includes those who do data entry, write descriptive content, rehouse material, and review final products. It's best to list by role (or title) and not personal name since that may change—especially when working with interns, students, or volunteers who are often employed on an as-needed basis.

Matching tasks to roles

Match the checklist to the list of roles. Assign the tasks from the checklist to the proper party from the list of team members. Think about that person's function within the organization when dividing the work. For example, student assistants are great at helping with rehousing, giving the archivist more time to handle higher-level tasks such as investigating provenance or verifying rights transfer.

Drawing it

A workflow is a visual representation of your process that is clear and easy to understand. You can create a workflow with paper and pen, sticky notes, or use a software program such as Excel or Visio.

One way to sketch out a workflow is to draw a large shape (box, circle, oval) for each role. Leave room in the shape to include the tasks assigned to each role. If one role has multiple tasks that occur at different points in the accessioning process, break those tasks out and create two separate shapes for that role—one for each set of tasks. For example, the archivist may assign a reference code to a collection and then hand the material off to a student assistant for rehousing. After rehousing is complete the project passes back to the archivist to create a resource record. In that case, there will be three shapes: 1. Archivist = assign reference code. 2. Student assistant = rehouse. 3. Archivist = create resource record.

Now connect the shapes using arrows to illustrate the order of events. You may need to draw it a few times to get the sequence correct. Or you can use sticky notes to make rearranging easier.

Simple workflow diagram

Example workflows:

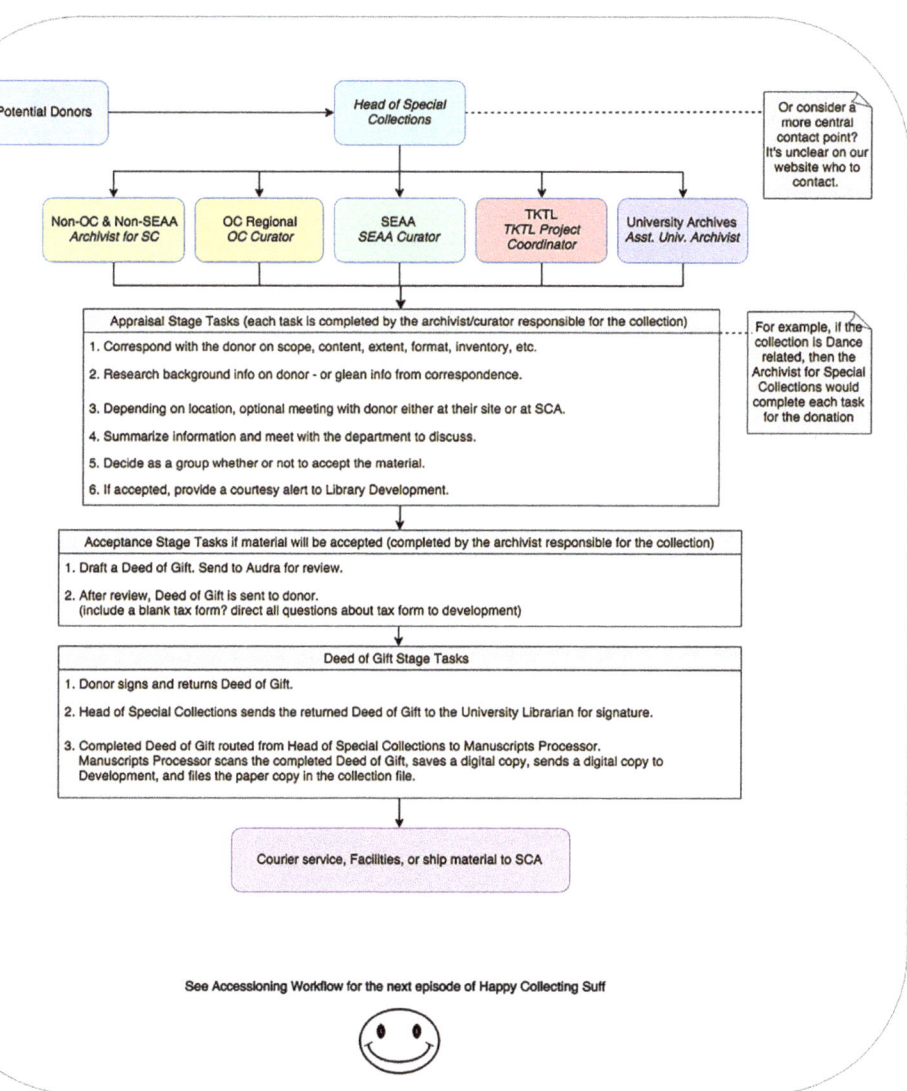

Donor Relations Workflow. University of California, Irvine. Kelly Spring & Krystal Tribbett.

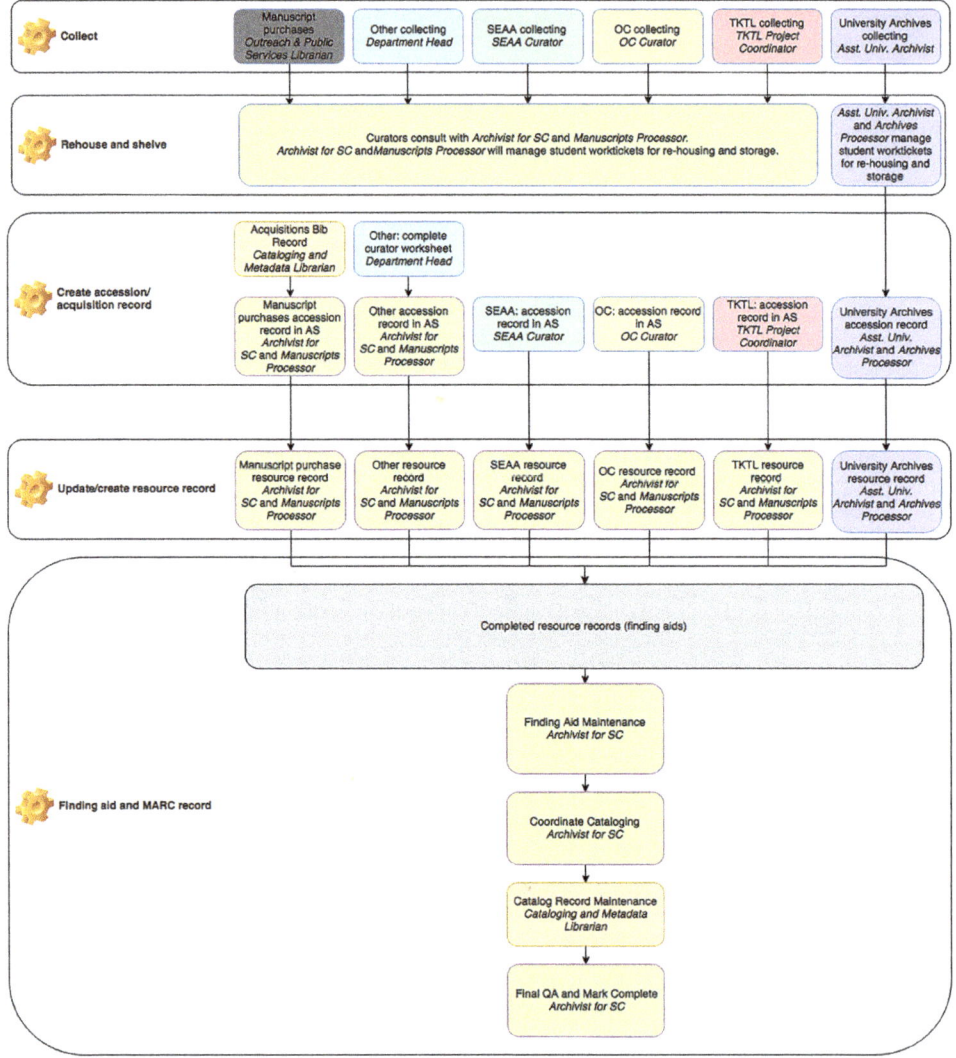

Accessioning Workflow. University of California, Irvine. Kelly Spring.

Researcher Request

Patron requests access to an accession or an unprocessed protion of a collection.

Identifying Materials

Senior Reference Archivist works with the patron to determine which boxes are of most interest.

Ideally, we already have box level inventories. If not, the Manuscripts Archivist will provide as much information as possible.

Processing

Once the boxes have been identified, the Senior Reference archivist passes along the request to the Manuscripts Archivist.

Manuscripts Archivist requests the boxes and oversees processing.

Once processing is complete the Manuscripts archivist alerts the Senior Reference Archivist.

Access

Senior Reference Archivist contacts the patron and arranges the research visit.

Process-on-Demand Workflow. Johns Hopkins University. Kelly Spring.

Project Plans

When you started this journey, you created an inventory. Now that you know exactly what needs to happen to every collection in that inventory, how will you manage them in total? This is where the last piece comes in: the project plan. The project plan is similar to a dashboard in that it gives a single, large-scale picture of all the progress being made on your backlog. The project, in this sense, refers to the overall activity designed to produce your baseline product. And the plan defines the approach you will use to get each collection to that baseline. To create a project plan, you will combine the inventory with the workflow.

Benchmarks

If you created your inventory using a spreadsheet, create a copy of your inventory and name it "project plan." Referring to your workflow, find the points where work is being handed off among team members. These points will now become benchmarks or deliverables. Devise a short title for each benchmark and note them in the project plan. In accessioning, these benchmarks include assigning an accession number and documenting where the material is stored. For processing, you may wish to choose data entry, rehousing, or finding aid publication as benchmarks. Add the benchmarks as new columns.

Overall status	Date of inventory entry.	Generally speaking, what is it?	Where did it come from?	Date the material arrived?	Accession number (Archivist)	Material rehoused? (student)

Sample project plan

Team members, if available, will want to focus on their particular task and not be distracted by what comes before or after their work. Go back to the benchmarks in your project plan and write down the roles assigned to each task (as seen in the example above). When used correctly, the project plan will easily show current work assignments.

Scalability

Start small with your project plan and modify if/when the scope expands. As long as the project plan is fluid, you can adjust to suit changing circumstances. What will remain unchanged, however, is the aim to reduce or eliminate your backlog by getting each collection to the baseline.

www.ingramcontent.com/pod-product-compliance
Lightning Source LLC
LaVergne TN
LVHW051228200326
834388LV00019B/1240

* 9 7 8 1 4 6 9 6 6 1 2 5 4 *